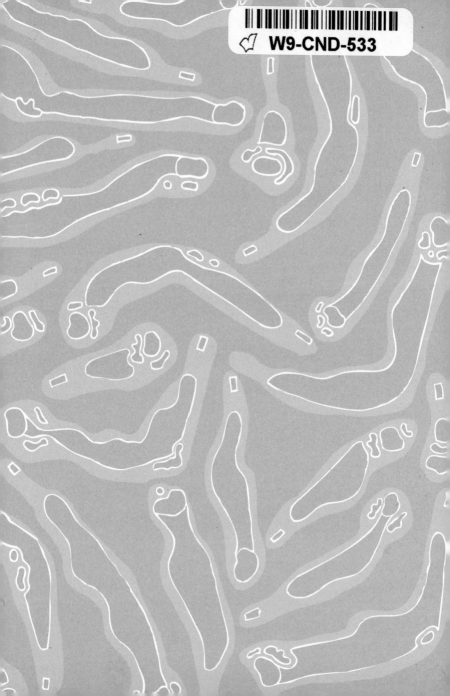

50 Reasons to **HATE**

and Why You Should **NEVER** Stop Playing!

Art Direction by Violet Lemay.
End Papers designed by Graham Fruisen.
Front and back cover scorecards provided by
Mark Evans and Gary Mclean.

**Library of Congress Cataloging-in-Publication
Data**

Names: Fruisen, Fred, author.
Title: 50 reasons to hate golf and why you should never
stop playing / by Fred Fruisen.
Other titles: Fifty reasons to play golf and why you
should never stop playing.
Description: First Edition. | Baltimore, MD : punchline.
[2017] | Includes bibliographical references and index.
Identifiers: LCCN 2016028145 | ISBN 9781938093869
(hardcover : alk. paper)
Subjects: LCSH: Golf—Anecdotes, facetiae, satire, etc.
| Golf—Humor.
Classification: LCC GV967 .F858 2017 | DDC
796.352—dc23
LC record available at https:
//lccn.loc.gov/2016028145

Printed in China

1 2 3 4 5 6 7 8 9 10

punchline

www.punchlineideas.com

50 Reasons to **HATE**

and Why You Should
NEVER *Stop Playing!*

Written and Illustrated
by FRED FRUISEN

Forward

by Chris Rodell

Author, Columnist, and Golf Fanatic

It's been calculated that every 4-hour round of golf involves about 13 minutes of actual golf. The rest of the time involves you trying to time your cough or fart perfectly with the backswing of your partner. So, even if you hate the actual time you spend golfing, it's really just little more than an intermission in a day that by any description is a whole lot of fun.

That's the joy of Fred Fruisen's delightful book. It captures with wit and euphoria why a game that confounds even the very best players can become a lifelong obsession for even the very worst golfers.

It reminds me of the exasperated golfer who after a particularly grinding hole blurted out, "And my wife thinks I'm out here having fun!"

I've come to realize that every round of golf includes one shot you'll likely remember for the rest of your life. The rest of the round might have been crap, but for that one moment you hit a shot that would make the greats of the game, like Ben Hogan, Tiger Woods, Rory McIlroy, or Lydia Ko, say, "Yes! That is how it's done!"

Perhaps devoted hackers might want to rethink the traditional way of scorekeeping. Instead of saying you shot a 105, you could tell everyone you shot a 6. That would be the total number of great shots you hit.

Golf is the only game that at its conclusion has a round-leveling forum that most consider a de facto part of the game itself: the 19th hole. It's where scratch golfers and high handicappers confer, commiserate, lament, or consecrate a round or a shot that might live forever.

Because when you've made it to the 19th hole, you've achieved something memorable. You've overcome countless logistical obstacles—you persevered through heartaches, rugged terrain, formidable hazards, and perhaps a few tee shots that didn't make it past the ladies' tee, leading to stinging ridicule that questions your manhood.

But you survived it all. In essence, you've won! Golf's not for the faint of heart. It's constructed to get each and every player to quit and go sun by the pool. So no matter what your score, you beat golf! Truly, it's something to celebrate.

I've been fortunate to have golf the way Fred describes it as a big part of my life, a life that's been filled up to the brim with fun, dashed expectations, and countless fond memories—an exuberant mirror of golf.

I'm a friend of the man who is the very essence of golf, Arnold Palmer. I've interviewed him more than 50 times. For the 15 summers I've known him, like clockwork he plays golf at Latrobe Country Club, across the street from his home, every day.

It's a great course, but it's the same course. I'll never forget the time I asked him why he plays his home course every single day of the summer. I said, "Laurel Valley is 20 minutes to the east, and Oakmont is just an hour to the west. Heck, if you wanted you could get in your jet and fly to Augusta, play 18 holes, and be back for dinner. Why do you always play Latrobe over and over?" "Well," he said, "it's just so close." What he was saying is he didn't want to waste time driving to play golf. He merely wanted to golf. As much as he could.

That's the feeling Fred Fruisen's book cultivates.

That's it. Golf in a nutshell.

"One reason golf is such an exasperating game is that a thing we learned is so easily forgotten, and we find ourselves struggling year after year with faults we had discovered and corrected time and time again."

— Bobby Jones

"Golf is not, and never has been,
a fair game."

— Jack Nicklaus

Golf: Torture or Pleasure?

I began playing golf with my parents when I was about seven. My mom was a very good golfer with a beautiful swing. She would always hit the ball long and straight. On the first tee she would surprise men who did not know her. Assuming she would hit a weak tee shot, their eyebrows would raise as she drilled a drive longer and much straighter than many of them could usually manage.

Dad on the other hand was wild. Most times he'd hit a sweeping hook. In spite of this pattern he would always seem to aim down the middle in hopes of producing the one shot out of ten that would go straight. He also had a fiery temper that wasn't conducive to playing a game that repeatedly tested his patience and constantly exposed his weaknesses.

I was lucky enough to inherit my mother's tempo and temperment. I remember countless times standing in the middle of the fairway at our balls with Mom, laughing at Dad as he attempted some ridiculous shot out of the deep woods. After the inevitable sound of his ball ricocheting off the trees, we'd hear his screams and curses of complete disbelief. He could be heard all over the course. In his eyes, golf was singling him out and picking on only him.

My father played every weekend, many times on both Saturday and Sunday. I often wondered why Dad continued playing a game that caused him so much anguish and so seldom rewarded his efforts.

Why do people like my father (there are millions of others exactly like him) devote so much of their spare time to a pursuit that infuriates them? Golfers are a unique breed of sportsmen who seem to enjoy, on some level, pain and failure.

When you think about it, golf is a pretty strange game. Its rules were developed centuries ago by shepherd and nobelmen alike. For some reason this casual pastime caught on and became a sport that is played with passion all over the world. The game is so gripping, the people who play it feel a deep attachment to golf as if they themselves invented it.

Golf may be more addictive than any other sport. The first time a golfer hits a great shot, the quest for more begins. Hitting the ball long and true feels so good that the golfer can never be satisfied. The feat must be repeated again and again, resulting in a lifelong quest that will consume a large portion of the golfer's thoughts, energy, and free time.

As a golf instructor for 20+ years, I have found I am as much a therapist and counselor as anything else. When people come to me they are rarely happy. Often they are frustrated, confused, and near the end of their golfing rope. It is up to me to help them out of their golf depression. We get to work right away on the physical parts of the game but more importantly, we work on the way they see the game and themselves and how the two can coexist in a somewhat productive and positive relationship.

I grew up loving golf and have been lucky enough to play and teach this crazy game all over the world. I get it. I love it, but it drives me crazy, too. That might be why I love it. I don't know. It's tough to understand exactly why. All I really know is that golf gives me great joy. Even when it makes me miserable. This game never ceases to surprise me with its beauty, its unpredictablity, and its predict-ability. There is no other sport like it.

50 Reasons to Hate Golf and Why You Should Never Stop Playing! explores many of the aspects of golf that drive us all nuts—and also why we love it so.

This is my love letter to golf.

~ Fred Fruisen

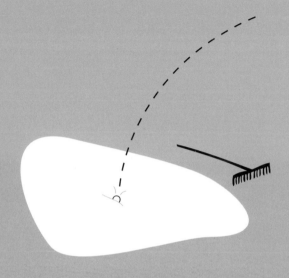

"Reverse every natural instinct
and do the opposite of what you
are inclined to do, and you will
probably come close to having
the perfect golf swing."
— Ben Hogan

"Golf is deceptively
simple and endlessly complicated;
it satisfies the soul and frustrates
the intellect. It is at the same
time rewarding and maddening —
and is without a doubt the greatest
game that mankind has
ever invented."

— Arnold Palmer

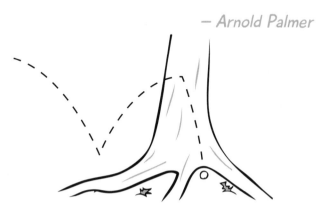

First Tee Jitters!

It's the first tee on a busy Saturday morning. The starter has just announced your group.

It's your turn. You're already nervous. You put the tee in the ground. You then notice the silence and look around. All eyes are on you. Your playing partners, the next group who just pulled up to the tee in their carts, everyone on the practice green.

Your hands begin to shake. You feel the blood draining out of your face. You question whether your legs can support you. You begin to sweat. Your heart is beating through your chest. You don't know if you are going to pee your pants or vomit, but something is about to come out of somewhere.

You pray to yourself, "I have no idea where this is going and I don't care, but *please* don't let me top it."

Just wanting it all to be over, you take a deep breath and swing...

Everybody Gets Them!

Even the pros get nervous on the first tee.

The difference is that the pros can channel those feelings in a positive way.

Most professionals want to feel that energy. The word they use instead of *nervous* is *excited*.

That Damn Ball!

The golf ball. It looks innocent, but it is not. It just sits there. Motionless. Mocking you. Daring you to hit it. You can almost see it giving you the finger. It's even more smug when it's on a tee.

The ball can't be trusted. It's evil. It will not obey.

This ball was created to torment you, yet you can't get enough. You try to love it, but you know in the end it will once again cause you pain and misery.

You want to hit that ball. Hurt it! Smash it so far there is no way it could still be round afterward.

The thing is, occasionally when you hit it, it obeys! So you chase after it thinking, "We're friends now, right?" Sure, it might play along for a few holes but you know deep down sometime soon it's going to fly away into the woods or decide it wants to go swimming right in the middle of your round.

I HATE YOU, BALL!

The Wonderous Orb!

Golfers hit a hard white ball that fits in their pocket, has more craters than the moon, and flies like a rocket. (I'm pretty proud of that one.)

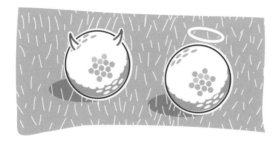

The golf ball not only symbolizes golf but everything that is good and holy in the world.

"Wanna go hit a bucket of balls?" This invitation is always met with the same level of enthusiasm as you asking your dog if he wants to go for a walk.

The night before a round, like kids we putt on the carpet imagining all the possiblities of the great moments we'll have tomorrow. This ball is magic!

The Hole Is So Tiny!

The object of golf is to hit a small ball into a tiny hole that is so far away, a stick with a flag on it is put in place just so you can see where it is. That's really small!

How is it that a game that is so vast and played over such a great area has a target so miniscule?

Who thought it would be fun to hit a ball through a field hundreds of yards long and try and find a hole smaller than this page? Why didn't the inventors of golf use a bigger hole? Like a bunker! Golf would be a lot easier! No more three putting!

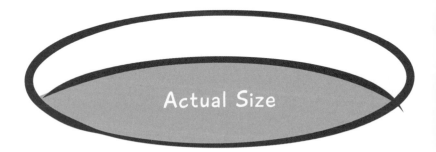

Actual Size

No Sport Is So Precise!

Golf has the smallest target in relation to its field than any other sport, by a longshot.

The cup is only 4.25 inches across, which is about the size of two and a half golf balls. Wow! The inventors of golf certainly wanted to create a challenging game! A very industrious greenskeeper could cut approximately 1,034,000 cups into the turf on an average (175-yard) par 3 hole. The same math in reverse applied to football would result in an end zone the size of a golf ball. Imagine that!

All golfers should be commended for finding a target so precise in such a timely manner. Add to that the fact that golfers repeat the same feat eighteen times over with all sorts of obstacles and terrain in about four hours. From a mathematical perspective, making a par or birdie is pretty remarkable. No wonder pars and birdies feel so good!

21

So Many Clubs!

Geez! Fourteen clubs!

The golf swing is so complex! You then have to figure out how to make your own idiosyncratic version of it work with fourteen different clubs!

Every club in the bag has a different length, size, shape, loft, and shaft.

Seems that after 500 years of ideas, hitting a golf ball would be a little simpler.

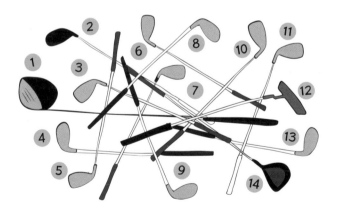

Technology!

For hundreds of years, inventors and engineers—even golfers in their garages—have toiled in an attempt to perfect fourteen golf clubs, one stick for every golfing task. The result of all of this hard work is a quiver full of weapons to take on golf's dragon: the Mighty Course.

It would be enough for craftsmen to design golf clubs to be functional, but these artisans have also made them beautiful. The sleek curves on a set of irons, the enticing angle and shape of the perfect wedge, the size and color of the head of a driver—any of this is enough to mesmerize the avid golfer.

Judging by the frequency with which most golfers purchase new clubs, it's safe to say they are highly coveted. When a new club appears in one of our friend's bag we can't resist holding it and wanting it in our bed...I mean, bag. Is it getting hot in here?

Gadgets!

After you buy clubs, the spending has just begun. You'll also need a golf bag, a bag for your golf bag (just in case you travel), a stroller for your bag so you can push your clubs around the course like a baby (because they are your babies), special shoes, a bag for your shoes, socks for each club, a brush to clean your clubs, golf tees, a tiny pitchfork for fixing ball marks, a special marker for writing on your ball, a special cup that fits over the ball so you can draw perfect lines on it, a laser range finder so you know the exact distance you are from the lake you're about to hit your ball into, and a ball retriever to rescue your ball from the lake.

Because of your obsession with golf, you'll play in any kind of weather, so you'll also need a golf umbrella, waterproof clothes, windproof clothes... and finally, a golf glove for only one hand.

A Golfer Is Always Prepared!

The very essence of the game is problem solving. Every shot requires the ultimate in cunning, creativity, and nerve. That creates a need for really cool gadgets!

The reason the golf bag has so many pockets is for stowing all of these very necessary tools so they are at the ready for any job or situation. Golfers are MacGyver, a Boy Scout, and James Bond all rolled into one.

It's So Freakin' Hard!

In order to just be *good* at golf, you have to master so many different skills: driving, putting, pitching, chipping, bunkers, irons, grip, swing plane, posture, hitting over water and under trees, drawing left, fading right, hitting it high and low, reading greens, judging wind, downhill, uphill, sidehill lies. And don't forget no two shots, holes, or courses are the same! Learning the rules and how to hit each club, and on and on. There is so much information to learn and remember!

In addition, countless thoughts are going through your head (none of them good) while you're trying to hit a tiny ball with a metal stick—with the hope that you'll actually be able to find it again.

Golf is schizophrenic. At times you are supposed to smash the ball as far as possible, and moments later you're meant to tap it only a few inches. All while trying not to break a rule or piss anyone off.

It's the Ultimate Challenge!

Golf is like a vampire: Once bitten you are never the same, and often you'll suck.

Why has golf endured for centuries? The allure is a mystery. Golf is seriously *hard*. However, humans enjoy being challenged. Golf satisfies that desire each and every round, and then some.

There is nothing quite like hitting a shot perfectly, playing a hole like a tour pro, or having shot your best score ever.

During each round you have many opportunities to see and feel perfection. Those moments are what draw us all to this fascinating and frustrating game.

Banana Slices and Duck Hooks!

It's so hard to get the ball to do what you want it to, when you want it to!

Others make driving the ball look so easy. The ball sails high, straight, and long. How boring!

For the rest of us golfers, the ball flies comically sideways. Drives fly every which way—more like trick shots. Hitting your ball with massé into the next fairway takes a lot of skill!

Why don't golf courses have holes that require you to hit really crooked shots?

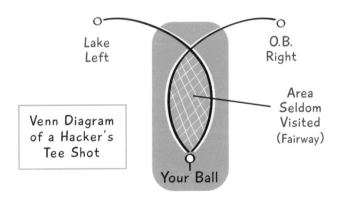

Lake
Left

O.B.
Right

Area
Seldom
Visited
(Fairway)

Venn Diagram
of a Hacker's
Tee Shot

Your Ball

Controlling Your Ball!

Golf is the only sport that allows a human to hurl, kick, throw, or hit an object such a great distance. This is perhaps the simplest explanation of why we have this obsession with playing golf.

It is a magical thing to see your ball climb and climb and fly so far from where it lay on the ground just moments before. Even better than hitting it far is the feeling you get when you have complete control over the flight of your ball. Controlling distance, direction, and trajectory—"working" the ball—curving it in the direction you desire at the moment you desire is the ultimate feeling of satisfaction for any golfer. It is both artistry and skill.

Launching the ball skyward is every golfer's chance to be Isaac Newton or the Wright brothers, to marvel at the hows and whys of gravity and how we in our own little way can better conquer it.

The #&%*# Putter!

There is a reason why you see hundreds of crazy-looking putters displayed in golf shops: it's because no one has ever been able to solve the riddle that is putting.

All golfers want to believe that there is a putter out there that will cure their putting woes. This mythical, illusive club is the Holy Grail of golf. Does it really exist?

Club designers have tried every possible head size, shape, and material conceivable, stuck it on the end of a shaft, and called it a putter. Golfers rush out to try the latest "magic wand," only to be disappointed. Alas, the quest continues.

Give it up! If there was a putter out there that truly worked better, everyone would use it.

Still skeptical? Then ask any golfer you know: *How many putters do you own?*

When You Finally Find "The One."

When you see a golfer with an old putter you can almost be assured that he/she can putt really well. This golfer and putter have been together a long time. The putter has nicks and marks from decades of rounds, both good and bad. The grip fits its owner's hand just right. There is trust. One never blames the other when things aren't going well.

Much like a family member, this club is irreplaceable. If ever lost, it would leave a hole in the heart.

The Little Shots!

Golf is the most disheartening game because in two shots you can advance the ball 400+ yards, land on or near the green, and then take four more shots from close range to get the ball in the hole.

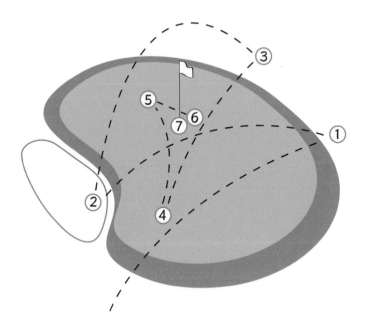

The Game Within the Game!

It's just not enough to hit the ball well in golf. Learning to score is the game within the game.

Scoring takes technique, cunning, perseverance, and some creativity. Learning what to do and, more importantly, what not to do at the correct moment is essential if you want to score your best.

Golf sometimes rewards good shots; sometimes golf rewards bad shots. Yep, even bad shots.

The secret of scoring is not in the mammoth drives or towering iron shots. It is in the little shots—the shots from 30 yards and closer to the green.

Not all approach shots will find their target. The sign of an accomplished golfer is in his or her ability to cover up those mistakes with quality pitching, consistent chipping, and reliable putting.

If you want a better score, fall in love with practicing the little shots on and around the greens.

Bad Breaks!

"Golf is brutal! This game seems to have it out for me! I get absolutely no breaks!"

It's so unfair that a perfectly struck shot hits the fairway, catches a slope, then trickles into a lake.

Golf is a rat bastard!

Good Breaks!

Most of the bad breaks golfers complain about are self-inflicted; for example, attempting low percentage shots or simply not hitting the right club.

Some golfers are like investors. They try to play the odds and patiently maneuver their way around the golf course. Other golfers are risk takers. They like the thrill of pulling off the great shot. Like a gambler, these golfers can win big and also lose big. Each golfer has to decide which way to play.

Golfers usually create their breaks, whether good or bad. Golf rewards good decisions and punishes bad ones. If you are able to remain disciplined, more times than not, the breaks will go your way.

World-famous sports psychologist Bob Rotella said it best: "The best way to shoot lower scores is to avoid shooting higher ones."

That is always a recipe for success.

Doin' Time!

At some point every golfer finds him- or herself in a situation where there is little chance of escape. It is called-*jail*. It's usually dark and wet in there, and you're not getting out anytime soon. When you find yourself in jail, the penalty is usually severe.

Attempting the Impossible!

So, you're in jail. No big deal!

Here is the situation: A wild tee shot has left you deep in the woods, about 170 yards from the green. There are only about 15 trees between you and an opening the size of a basketball, about 30 yards away. If you can keep it low with a little fade and *then* have it rise, you know you can keep it in the air long enough to carry the lake in front of the green, where the pin is tucked behind a bunker.

It doesn't matter that Tiger Woods has failed at easier shots. The same laws of physics don't apply to you and your 24 handicap skill set. Not to mention you have all the technology that your recently acquired garage sale five iron has to offer.

You're only 8 over after five holes. The odds are clearly in your favor. You've got this shot! Because in golf, possiblities outweigh probabilities!

Why a Stupid Hole?

Why a hole? Why do we want the ball to end up underground? Can it be because we hate the ball and want to kill it and bury it? So many questions...

The Hole Story!

About 500 years ago, a shepherd somewhere in Scotland was bored and started hitting small stones with his crook across his pasture to pass the time. The idea quickly caught on with other shepherds. This eventually grew into a somewhat organized activity with rocks being replaced by other "balls" that would fly farther through the air. The object of this new game was to have the ball end up in a small hole. That hole was a rabbit's hole.

Pastures were large, and rabbit holes were plentiful, so it wasn't hard to fashion an entire course.

Interestingly, a rabbit will always dig its hole in the middle of the nicest, greenest patch of grass. That is not only how the golf hole came to be, but the golf green as well.

Golfers owe a debt of gratitude to the rabbit. Oh yeah, and to the shepherds, also.

The Green Monsters!

Golfers hit a tiny ball that curves every which way with clubs that send the ball every which way over hundreds of yards of turf, woods, traps, and whatever crap is thrown in their way. Then after too many shots, and intensely frustrated, they arrive at the green. The game completely changes. It's almost like golf is saying, "Now let's *really* piss them off!"

So after wailing at the ball like cavemen for 15 minutes they're now required to "tap" the ball with the force of a feather because the grass on the green is cut so short the ball won't stop rolling! That's not enough, though. Now golf says, "If we put crazy slopes everywhere to make the ball roll even faster *and* sideways, maybe we'll see a nervous breakdown today!" And that's *still* not enough! To make it even harder, the hole is moved every other day so that no one can figure out how to solve this f#%*ing riddle!

Magic Carpets!

How do greenskeepers do it? They truly are the unsung heroes of golf. Greenskeepers go to work each day long before sunrise so that the course is ready for *you*. These devoted souls grow and maintain greens that are remarkably smooth in spite of the beating that the surfaces take each day.

The reputation of a course is largely determined by the quality of its greens.

Do your part to help by repairing your ball marks. And on occasion, thank your greenskeeping staff for their hard work.

Sand Pits from Hell!

Golf is a very difficult game that subjects you to some pretty humiliating situations. Bunkers are special places that are designed to make you look even more foolish.

Greenside sand traps provide you the opportunity to stand alone in a pit while everyone in your group watches you flail hopelessly at your ball.

This shot is terrifying because two of its three possible outcomes are bad:

1) You fail to get out. S@#%! You have to do it again! And perhaps AGAIN! This dramatically increases the odds of the next bad thing happening.

2) You catch it thin, and the ball sails almost on to the next hole, which guarantees to put you in an impossible situation.

3) A miracle! The ball ends up safely on the green. The golfing gods were with you...this time.

In the Beginning, There Were Bunkers!

Sheep were the first golf course architects. They would dig holes in pastures and hills to shield themselves from the wind and rain.

If you are ever driving around sheep country (Scotland, Ireland, or New Zealand), notice the beautifully dug bunkers dotting the fields and hills.

This history lesson won't improve your bunker play, but it's nice to know that sand traps weren't the invention of a sadistic designer whose only desire was to punish golfers.

Hazards!

Sand traps, lakes, out of bounds...Why does there have to be so much stuff in the way on a golf course?

Isn't golf hard enough? Just trying to hit the ball in the direction you want is a formidable challenge!

Golf courses should be like fields in other sports: flat and free of any obstacles that get in the way.

Even then the game would be no picnic.

Gorgeous Landscape!

There is little debate that the beauty of a golf course is unmatched in sport. The source of much of that beauty comes from the hazards.

Each golf course is a work of art. The finest examples, courses like Pebble Beach, Augusta National, or St. Andrews, look as if they were designed by God himself.

When arriving at a new course, it is picturesque and inviting. You have a strong desire to get out there and experience the course firsthand.

Then while actually playing the course, your attitude can change. Something you once thought beautiful is now not quite so appealing.

During your occasional unwanted visits into the hazards, keep your perspective and remember to appreciate those gleaming white sand bunkers and beautiful blue lakes.

All the Friggin' Rules!

Don't we already have enough rules in our lives? Do you really want to spend your free time playing a game that requires an advanced degree to understand its rules?

The rules of golf are so complicated that they fill a 200-page book. In addition to that, there is 750-page companion book called *The Decisions on the Rules of Golf* to help you decipher the original *Rules of Golf*. No joke!

The rules of golf are so complicated that the tour professionals—the best players in the world—don't know them! Every week in professional tournaments, players are either penalized or even kicked out of the tournament for breaking a rule they didn't know or were unable to understand.

What chance does the average golfer have if the top golfers on the planet can't figure them out?

The Rules Are Your Friend!

Sure, there are a lot of rules but once you understand the thought behind them, you'll realize that many of the rules help save you strokes and help you when you find yourself in unfair situations.

In a game where no two shots are ever the same, it is necessary to have rules that cover an almost infinite number of outcomes.

Divots!

Y ou're playing great and smoke a drive right down the middle of the fairway on the 12th hole. Everyone in your group knows you're on fire today.

When you get close to your ball, your heart sinks. It's lying in the %@#$*! middle of huge crater!

You do the best you can, but with that lie you literally have no chance. You end up with a triple bogie and now the rest of your round is ruined!

Why should someone be penalized for hitting the perfect golf shot right down the fairway?

Golf is so unfair!!

Play It as It Lies!

One of the original rules of golf written in the mid-1700s states, "Play the ball as it lies."

It's an important rule because if you were able to improve your lie, then to what extent? How far could you move the ball? If you could move out of a divot, then why wouldn't it be okay to move out of tall grass or water or sand? Or from behind a tree? Where would it end?

Really, without this rule there would be no game.

The fact is that *every* golfer's ball will end up in a divot, and not just once in a while; this is a pretty regular occurrence. The beauty of golf is that all golfers must deal with whatever is presented to them. No exceptions.

The best advice is for everyone to be mindful about filling their own divots. The round you could be saving might very well be your own.

Handicaps!

The handicap is a way to *officially* remind you of how inadequate your skills are as a golfer.

The handicap is also a barometer used to screen potential playing partners. Roughly translated, "What's your handicap?" means, "Do I want to play with you or not?"

When asked for his handicap, a good player knows his index to the decimal: "I'm a 5.21."

A high-handicap golfer isn't quite so precise. He responds, "I'm *about* a 24." Translation: "I'm a 30."

Name Joseph A. Hacker   GHIN

Golfing Handicap Indication Number

Club: Bushwood CC   Your Official Rating: **YOU SUCK !**

Number of Scores Posted 161

SCORE HISTORY – MOST RECENT FIRST * IF USED

1	99*	97	102*	100*	103*
6	106	98	111	97*	99*
11	101*	106*	96*	102*	109*
16	103*	99*	108*	104*	106*

No Sport Is as Fair!

The beauty of golf is that anyone of any level can have a fair game with anyone of any level.

You can't do that in any other sport. Granddads can't play a fair game of football with their grandkids, but in golf, a professional and a 15 handicap amateur can have a very spirited match. The pro would even stand a very good chance of losing!

Handicaps also make pairing partners in tournaments fair. If not for this, the same predictable people would always win. Handicapping is one of golf's wonderful assets; it makes the game fair and fun for everyone.

Handicaps are complex. They take into account a player's ability to score and other factors such as how difficult or easy a course is to play. This system ensures that golfers from anywhere in the world are playing the same game with consistent standards.

What Am I, Hunting Bigfoot?

High-handicap golfers spend a lot of time *not* playing the golf course. Instead, they get to explore the periphery, the scrub, the land the course designer decided was not suitable for a golf hole.

In fact, the higher your handicap, the more alone time you get in the deep woods amongst the woodland creatures and reptilia, searching for a small white ball. While your playing partners stand on the fairway tanning themselves, you pace back and forth through thorns, poison ivy, and muck.

Finding a golf ball in a maze of trees and leaves isn't accomplishment enough, though. It has to be *your* ball or it doesn't count.

If you're lucky enough to find it, you have to play the ball from whatever absurd position it's in, then it might take you a million strokes to get it out.

Yeah, that sounds fun!

You Get to Enjoy Nature!

There is absolutely nothing better than being outside on a beautiful day on a golf course. You get to play on cleverly sculpted grounds away from the troubles of your life. Hearing the birds, feeling the breeze, and smelling the grass is like heaven. Even if you do play poorly.

All the Walking!

The last thing you want to do is walk five miles up and down hills (it always seems like a lot more up than down) for four hours, either carrying thirty pounds of metal on your back or pushing a silly trolley. All this to search for a little white ball and to end up right back where you started.

A Leisurely Stroll!

Is there anything better than walking the course on a crisp morning or late afternoon when everything is still and the sun is low?

This is a little piece of heaven, the way life was meant to be!

It's even better when you can go out and play alone. That is when you can truly understand what this magical game is all about.

When you get to play by yourself, free of distractions, you seem to completely relax and feel the course as a living, breathing thing. You become in tune with the course and what it requires of you.

These are the times when you truly get it.

Notice when you see someone come off the golf course in the late afternoon after they've just played alone. They always seem to be smiling like they've just been let in on a wonderful secret.

Cheaters!

Golfers seem to be really bad at math. How hard is it to count up to 6 or 7?

Everyone knows you moved your ball on the 8th hole, and all day you keep saying you made a four when you really took five.

You've got honesty issues. Where else in your life are you cheating?

Golfers' Math 101

3 shots + 3 putts = 5
3 shots + 2 putts = 4
2 shots + 2 putts = 3

When in doubt say,
"Put me down for a bogie."

"*Golfers*" *Don't Cheat!*

Integrity is the number one core value in the game of golf. Having to do the right thing even though there aren't any referees around is part of what makes golf unique in sport.

People who cheat might "play golf," but they are not "golfers." There is a huge difference. True golfers always do the right thing even if it hurts, and it usually does for a short while. Then pride follows. It is like the adage: short-term pain, long-term gain.

If you cheat and don't get caught, you win a hollow victory and what else—a five-dollar bet? If you do get caught, and you eventually will, you will have lost respect and credibility for a very long time. Once found out, it's almost impossible to shed the reputation of being labeled a cheat. It's not worth it.

You become a true "golfer" the first time you call a penalty on yourself. It is a badge of honor.

Three-Footers!

This seems to be the hardest shot in golf.

You are so close to the hole you can see the bottom of the cup, yet the hole looks smaller to you now than it did from 200 yards.

Wasn't the gimme invented so that golfers wouldn't have to look like idiots taking three putts from two and a half feet?

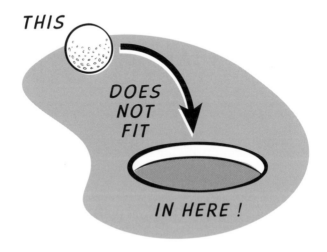

THIS

DOES NOT FIT

IN HERE !

Real Golfers Always Putt Out!

The short putts are the ultimate test of nerves.

Making three-foot putts is a skill just as important and impressive as driving the ball 300 yards.

How many times have you seen a major championship decided by a player making or missing a three-foot putt? How about *every one*?

Gimmes are only allowed if you are playing in match play. Then your opponent can choose to concede a putt to you. Picking up your ball before it is holed in stroke play is equal to quitting a hole.

In baseball, we don't assume a man on third will make it home. In football, when a team gets to the 5-yard line, the official doesn't say, "Close enough. Touchdown!"

Hearing the sound of the ball hitting the bottom of the cup is your reward for completing the hole.

And it also happens to be the object of the game.

Friggin' Etiquette!

Golf etiquette is the set of manners every golfer is expected to instinctively know without ever being taught. They are the secret unwritten rules for a game that already has too many rules.

Just trying to keep your ball on the course makes golf tough enough. Now you have the extra pressure of acting politely as you make an eight on a par 3.

"Don't stand there!" "Be quiet!" "Stop moving!" Not knowing proper etiquette makes you feel like a child being disciplined by your mom in church. It's awkward and uncomfortable, and people notice.

How do you know if you've breached a rule of golf etiquette? First, everything seems to come to a screeching halt. Then a noticeable silence overcomes the group, followed by whispers. Finally, everyone is glaring at you as if you are a puppy who has just pooped on the living room carpet.

Consideration for Others Is Important!

Dude! Your shadow is blocking the hole!

Society would benefit greatly if people would conduct themselves as politely and civilly as they do on the golf course.

Simple courtesies are what make life tolerable. Golf is a game that demands that you respect its rules and also the people who play it with you.

Etiquette may seem like a pain, but in the end, we all benefit from people being respectful of one another. How can that be a bad thing?

The Foul Language!

Wait a minute. Isn't golf supposed to be a game of etiquette and civility?

What is it about golf that turns anyone who plays into a potty mouth? As soon as the first drive is struck, all participants seem to develop a special temporary strain of Tourette's syndrome.

Golf courses look serene and idyllic, with grand clubhouses, beautiful grounds, and well-dressed people. How is it then that this is the setting for such foul and disgusting language?

Beginning at daybreak on weekend mornings you will hear the cries of distress and screams of frustration wafting up through the trees.

Golfers are the birds of the golf course, and obscenities are their song.

Is this a game, or are people being tortured?

Colorful Articulation!

If swearing were an art form, then the golf course would be its canvas.

The creative use of language and the willingness to share with all, even from five holes away, never fail to impress on the course. Some golfers can't break 90, but they play to scratch when it comes to profanity. As the golfer watches his ball fly into the lake that once again collects his ball, his obscenity-laced tirade can be heard from off in the distance.

Appreciate his work. He is a true artist.

Drinking and Driving Is Legal?

Can golf really be considered a sport if you are drinking while you're playing it? Wouldn't that put golf on par with bowling?

At a golf course, rules matter. You'll get in serious trouble if you break a club rule or the rules of golf; however, federal and state laws aren't quite so important. At a golf course, it's legal to drink and drive—as long as you wear a collared shirt.

It's strange. No one really seems to mind if you are drinking while operating a golf cart. Perhaps it's because carts don't have doors or seatbelts, or maybe it's because the windshield is made of plastic.

If you want to see grown men regress into 10-year-old boys driving bumper cars at the state fair, give them a few beers, put them behind the wheel of a golf cart, and watch them race down the fairway.

Is this a golf course or a frat house?

Golf + Beer = Awesome!

Can this be true? Is this heaven?

Not only can you drink while you play, a cute girl in short shorts comes to *YOU* on the course every few holes and asks if you want more beer!

And the answer is always, "YES! We definitely want more beer!"

Faster!!!
You can make it!
I LOVE GOLF!!!

Semipublic Urination!

Bathrooms are merely a concept on the golf course. Most times, anything goes! Semipublic urination is as common as swearing after your tee shot.

This is almost exclusively a guy thing. Once outside, men seem to turn into dogs. As soon as golfers tee off, bladders shrink and the need and frequency of "having to go" increases dramatically. As the round progresses the golfer becomes more comfortable in his surroundings, becomes less inhibited, and pees wherever he pleases. The course is now seen as his turf. His desire to "mark" his territory is rivaled only by that of his playing partners.

Trees, rocks, neighboring yards, rose bushes, golf carts—nothing is off limits (unless it's really high). Golfers become so lazy that even if there is a restroom within sight, it's not close enough. It can't wait. It's always, "I've got to go, now!"

Ur-ine Control Now!

Yippee! We can go when we want, where we want, as much as we want! The golf course is the only place where we have the freedom to whiz in plain view of million-dollar properties without fear of having the authorities called.

Freedom! No, let's call it, PEE-dom!

Rejoice and unite, golfers! Whip it out! Pee proud! Come out from behind your tree. Wee for all to see!

Playing with the Boss...You're Screwed!

Y ou've noticed that your boss is a golf nut. In trying to forge a relationship with him you have mentioned more than once that you love golf, too. Week after week you exchange highlights of your rounds. He admits he is a solid 14 handicap. You, on the other hand, have innocently exaggerated your skills. Now he's under the impression that your handicap is in the single digits, although you struggle to break 100.

On Wednesday the boss informs you he has signed you up to be the A player in a corporate event with him and some business associates. The tournament is Friday, less than 48 hours away.

Uh oh...Unless there is a miracle in your bag, come Monday he'll never look at you the same again.

Cancel all meetings! Must google "golf tips"! YOU'RE SO SCREWED!...SCREWED!!!

Golf and Business!

People in the business world who play golf have a competitive advantage over those who don't. Golf is an invaluable tool for networking and socializing. It's well known that a great deal of business is conducted at the golf course.

Golf reveals the true character and ethics of individuals. Trust is paramount in business.

AND best of all, if you play golf, many times you'll be invited by business associates to play during the week instead of being stuck in the office!

What Is This, Secret Code?

Mulligan, bogie, dogleg, birdie, eagle, flop shot, skull, horseshoe, shank, duff, whiff, gimme, hog back, divot, slice, hook, snowman.

Golf terms sound more like nicknames of people you'd meet in prison.

Golf Jargon!

Golf has its own weird, wonderful language.

Common golf terms sound like gibberish to a non-golfer. Have some fun and see if your non-golfing friends can translate the following:

"When I turned I had a couple of tweet-tweets then I got on the bogie train."

"I tried to cut the dogleg, hit a hozel rocket, and went O.B. Then I horseshoed for a quad."

"I hoofed it with the dew scrappers and the flat bellies. One guy only hit duck hooks, banana balls, and worm-burners."

"I had a fried egg and ended up with a snowman."

"My handicap is scratch from the tips."

"Three jacks are killing me! Not to mention I keep blading my chips and skulling my hybrid."

"My big stick has an extra stiff shaft."

Sounds pretty crazy, huh?

The Clothes!

W hat's with golf fashion? It's either really boring or makes people look like clowns.

A Classic Look!

A golf shirt and trousers or Bermuda shorts is a classic look that never goes out of style. When people dress like golfers they look sporty, casual, and classy all at the same time. Need proof?

1) A teenage boy dressed in golf attire is a breath of fresh air compared to the usual fashion decisions made by members of this generation.

2) Women look more youthful and athletic in their color-coordinated outfits and visors.

3) The term "business casual" could really refer to golf attire—comfortable and not too formal.

You can always tell a golfer walking around town. They look neat, groomed, and ready for a round.

If you want a photo of you to look good 20 years from now, dress in classic golf attire.

Fashion tip: Try and take it easy on loud colors and crazy patterns.

The Wanna-Be Tour Player!

Every club has a guy who looks "tour" but shoots about 95.

Here's how you recognize him: He doesn't work much because he's loaded. He's always at the course on weekdays. He dresses in very bright clothes that are a little too tight for his body shape. He has the latest equipment and a staff bag, and he rides alone in a golf cart even when he's playing in a foursome.

He either tops his drive on the first tee or slices it out of bounds, then takes a mulligan—or two.

Equal Ground!

Golf is the great leveling ground. Each player stands alone knowing his weaknesses, and in spite of them, negotiates to the best of his ability whatever obstacles golf puts before him.

Nothing can change or influence situations you are presented with by golf: not status in the community, money, or past circumstances. Golf doesn't care who you are. You could be a millionaire or Joe Average. Only you and your own abilities determine the outcome. In this way, golf is pure.

Each player has the same simple task—to get the ball in the hole—and that is a beautiful thing! On the course, all are equal. Everyone who plays with grit, determination, and honesty is respected and valued equally. Many times on the course you will see people from completely different social circles playing together. Where else in life is this the case?

Golf Tips from a Hacker!

Every club has one: A guy who can't break 90 but constantly gives swing advice and detailed analysis about everything you are doing wrong. He knows exactly what your problems are but hasn't got a clue about how to fix his own.

Gotta Love Him!

Yep, every club has one.

"Joe Hacker" is a golf enthusiast in the truest sense of the word. He lives to play golf and is in a constant battle to improve but doesn't see results.

His enthusiasm is such that he needs to share his wealth of knowledge with others—namely, you. In fact, you have become one of his pet projects.

This guy always seems to get paired with you or asks you if you want to play together.

Here is how to spot Joe Hacker:

You'll often see him on the practice areas teaching some guy he has just met. During his unsolicited demonstrations, Joe Hacker hits a 30-yard slice but still considers himself an expert on how to hit a soft high draw.

He's a good enough guy. He means well and he loves golf, so you've gotta love him.

Geezers!

Want to feel extra pressure while on the course? Try to stay ahead of a group of senior golfers.

This army of old guys plays *so fast*—even though they are ancient, *and* they are also walking and pulling their clubs. Where did all this energy come from? Are their hip and knee replacements bionic?

And if you hold them up they get really aggressive and start yelling at you and calling you names from 100 yards away.

Even though they just bunt it, they still can't see where the ball ends up. They just walk down the middle of the fairway. They carry 14 clubs but only use five—a driver, hybrid, 7 iron, wedge, and putter.

Why do old golfers want to play 18 holes in two and a half hours? What is their hurry? Where do they have to go? Or do they really have to *GO*, if you know what I mean.

Better with Age!

Time has taken away the senior golfers' ability to hit it as far as they once did, but it hasn't taken away their competitiveness, their cunning, nor their surprisingly razor-sharp short game skills.

Playing with seniors will teach you many things, like adapting, playing to your strengths, how to chip and putt—*and* how to keep up the pace of play. One thing is for sure: you'll hear some great stories!

Slow Players!

Oh, my God! Can we get it moving?!

This is not life or death, people! Do you really need five minutes to line up your putt? The fate of all mankind does not hinge on you making this four-foot putt to shoot 93!

Please, we are all begging you, HIT THE BALL!

45 Seconds Is a Long Time!

Golf is meant to be relaxing. You've worked hard all week and it's your chance to unwind and enjoy yourself. It's okay to take time to make sure you have gone through your pre-shot routine.

Taking extra care before a shot will produce better results, which will ultimately save time.

Just make sure you are moving at a pace that is taking into consideration others in your group and groups behind you.

The rules of golf allow players 45 seconds to hit their shot once it is their turn.

If you are holding up a group behind you, wave them through. There is no need to feel rushed. It will only lead to more mistakes and slower play.

By the way, slow play doesn't necessarily come from high-handicap golfers. Everyone needs to do their part to keep the pace of play moving.

Playing Through!

You're playing as a single and you've been waiting on every shot for six holes because the group in front of you is hacking it around.

Your displeasure is made conspicuous by your posture as you stand in fairways and on tee boxes leaning on your club—the classic golf, "Excuse Me?!" They finally notice and wave you up to the green.

Suddenly, you feel yourself tighten up. Uh oh. Now there is pressure and expectation.

You rush and hit an awful shot short and right. You feel like an idiot, so you hurry to your ball and without thinking, you blade a pitch over the green.

Impressive! You follow that shot by chunking a chip, barely making the green. Now you're so embarrassed, you blast your 20-footer 10 feet past the hole.

Humiliated, you pick up without holing out, slink away, and pray you never see them again.

Waving You Up!

Golf is a game of manners, and one of the benefits of golf etiquette is that it allows faster players to play through slower groups. It's a courtesy that makes the game more enjoyable for everyone.

Take your time, though; in the end it will save strokes and your ego.

Ranger Danger!

Yeah, this guy is the golf Nazi who rushes you around the course.

He's the old guy whose sole purpose in life is to hassle you while you're trying to have fun. He takes his job way too seriously and has gone power mad.

Of course you could be playing great the entire round and never see him, but as soon as you hit one poor shot or have a bad hole you can be guaranteed he'll appear in his cart and scowl at you as if you're the only reason the entire course is backed up.

He'll bark at you and say something insightful like, "You guys are going to have to pick up the pace."

Sure, that helps. How can we play faster if we can't keep from hitting our balls sideways?

If you want us to play faster, ranger man, how about giving us a tip that will keep us from losing eight balls a round!

The Lonely Ranger!

The ranger isn't the most popular guy at the golf course. He's got a tough job. He is dealing with dozens of groups and is trying to keep pace of play moving so that everyone on the course—including you!—can enjoy their day a little more.

Just smile and say, "Yes, sir, thank you, sir. You're doing a great job!"

It Takes So Long!

Golf is an all-day affair. You drive to the course, warm up, play for four or five hours, and then sit at the 19th hole talking about what you just did.

If you don't want to spend your entire day off playing a round of golf, you'll have to wake up at 5 a.m. so you can tee off at first light.

While most others are still in bed you'll be well on your way, displaying how much of an ass you can make of yourself both athletically and emotionally. Then you can go home and mow the lawn! Perfect!

I Wish the Sun Would Never Set!

Is there a better way to spend a day?

You are away from the usual pressures of everyday life; away from traffic, computers, and boring obligations that steal your rare "Me" time.

Now you are outside breathing fresh air, walking with friends, talking about whatever, and giving each other the business. You all share in a common struggle with no real-world consequences. You're not playing to keep your tour card. If you screw up, who cares? Ultimately, golf is just a game.

Each time you tee it up, something amazing might happen. At the very least, something funny or tragic (same thing) will happen that you will all talk about later.

You might as well play because if you don't, you'll get hassled into doing some awful chore or end up sitting on your butt watching golf on TV.

A Channel Just for Golf?...Really?

Since the introduction of the Golf Channel in 1995, the level of tension at home between spouses has increased dramatically.

Broadcasts of everything golf 24/7! You can see every tournament in the freakin' world! You'll see golf tips, golf morning shows, golf news, golf infomercials, golf reality shows, movies about golf!

Oh, my God! Get a LIFE!

Our Prayers Have Been Answered!

For the hard-core golf addict, while at home, Golf Channel is the drug of choice.

This is the channel to watch if you want others to leave the room. It clears the den faster than burrito farts. It is your all-purpose "leave me alone" move.

Just click the remote. Instant peace and quiet.

Keeping up to date on the world of golf is essential. Golfers have to know if Rory is arriving at the US Open a day early or if Jordan Speith is wearing blue on Saturday at the John Deere Classic. This isn't just entertainment! It's research, dammit!

Golf Channel is CNN, History Channel, ESPN, and the Home Shopping Network all rolled into one.

The rest of the family is on their own. The den belongs to you this day, and most every other day.

Besides, where else are you going to see rebroadcasts of the final round of the '86 Masters?

Teaching Your Wife to Play!

Are you insane? You have to be either the bravest or stupidest man alive to attempt such a feat. Trying to teach your wife to play golf is a suicide mission. There can be no positive outcome. Many have tried, none have come back the same.

Go ahead, tell her what she should and shouldn't be doing every minute and see how long it takes before she tries to hit *your* balls with a 7 iron.

Playing Partner!

Lucky is the man whose wife enjoys golf.

It would be wise, though, to leave her golfing tutelage to the professionals. But you can't put a price on having a partner who shares and/or understands your borderline obsession with the game.

Golf is the perfect activity for couples. You can play together, or she can play with her friends! And now when you travel you won't have to beg to play golf while on vacation! Jackpot!

If you play your cards right, watching golf might become another shared hobby. The ultimate would be sitting on the couch with your sweetie munching on pimento cheese sandwiches while watching the back nine on Masters Sunday. Do you dare dream?

Best of all, you can get excited about gift shopping for her! Finally! You can pick something she'll like! You'll be a hero! You can even buy her shoes!

Where Did My Swing Go?

You practice and prepare for weeks. You feel you're really ready to play in the tournament.

For once, you're excited on the first tee! You feel you've really got a chance to do well, maybe even win your division! Confidently, you step up to the ball, go through your pre-shot routine, and swing...

"What the hell?!" Where in the world did that come from? You go to your bag to find another ball.

And for the rest of the day you play like you've never swung a golf club in your life.

Golf truly sucks.

Golf Is Fickle!

Putting together a good round of golf takes more than skill and dedication. Luck, creativity, the ability to overcome adversity, decision making, patience, and mental fortitude all play a major role.

Just hitting good shots doesn't guarantee success. Every golfer has said at some time, "I hit the ball really well today, but I couldn't score."

It's hard to put a finger on exactly what it is that helps you score, but we know it's called *scoring*.

Some rounds we score when we are swinging well; other times we score when we are hacking it around.

This mysterious aspect of golf is part of its charm. In golf, you don't always get what you deserve. Sometimes you get burned without deserving it, and sometimes you come out smelling like a rose when you should have been hammered.

The Golfing Gods are a fickle bunch.

It's SO Frustrating!

Why is it so hard to hit a ball that isn't moving? You're even looking at it the entire time!

Other sports are just the opposite of golf. The worse you are, the less you have to do it. In golf, the worse you are the *more* you have to do it. No one replaces you or says, "You're out!" You're required to continue the humiliation however long it takes.

How is it that others make it look so easy while your swing looks like a series of jerks and spasms resulting in your disappearance into the woods?

Hope you can swim, club!

It's SO Fun!

If you like puzzles or figuring out how to solve complicated problems, then golf is for you.

Each area of the game requires you to solve its unique set of complex problems in order to succeed.

For instance, putting couldn't be more different than driving a ball, but both are crucial skills to master if you want to have success.

(Interesting golf fact: If you were to compare the time it takes to swing a driver and a putter you would find that they take almost exactly the same amount of time.)

Then after you think you have mastered proper technique, golf provides you with literally an endless supply of new problems in the form of slopes, lies, courses, and atmospheric conditions.

All golfers are like mini scientists, trying to solve the ultimate riddle.

Training Aids!

Golfers are the most gullible, wishful, and desperate people in sports. They will purchase any product that claims it will help them shave a stroke or two off their score. Every crazy contraption conceivable is sold to these poor souls who long for a quick and easy cure for their poor technique.

Trained to Aid!

There are no shortcuts in golf and certainly there are no quick fixes. You can't buy your way out of poor fundamentals with something you saw on an infomercial at 2 a.m.

It is a fact that even with the explosion of technological advances in golf, in general, golf handicaps haven't improved in the past half century.

Quality golf swings and shots are born out of hard work and by engraining proper technique.

The good news is that *anyone* can improve their golf if they make the commitment to learn from a quality PGA teaching professional. Getting golf tips from your buddies who also struggle or using a gadget that promises instant results does not work.

If you learn golf properly your reward will be enjoying this great game for the rest of your life, instead of fighting it every day.

The Snowman!

The train-wreck hole. You know it's coming, your playing partners know it's coming, even the cart girl knows it's coming. The longer your round goes without your usual blowup, the more the pressure builds. You're like a ticking time bomb.

After the sudden burst of strokes and swearing, will you be able to recover or will another snowman arrive to wreck your scorecard—and your mood?

Pars, Birdies, and Eagles!

Par is the standard. It is the efficient completion of the hole without doing anything remarkable.

In golf, if you show discipline and skill and have a little luck, you can do better than is asked of you.

The birdie is the eraser that covers up past and future mistakes—it is the fuel that reenergizes and sometimes rescues your round. Eagles, if you can get them, are a rare glimpse into golfing perfection. The thrill of scoring under par, even if just for one hole, is immense. Once a golfer gets a taste, the desire to achieve more increases.

The great thing is, occasionally even average golfers get to experience pars, birdies, and eagles. Every round, most golfers play a hole, or at least hit a shot or a putt, as well as the world's best players. These shots, even if only by luck, are a wonderful gift that golf gives us all.

You Turn into a Crazy Person!

Why is it that you're a reasonable, controlled person in every aspect of life but when you get on the golf course you turn into a lunatic? You become an out-of-control, emotional, irrational rageaholic!

You *OFF* the Course

NICE GUY AWARD

You *ON* the Course

Golf Reveals the Real You!

With each and every shot, golf puts you in situations that will test you in a myriad of ways.

First, golf tests your ability to control yourself physically. Can you make the proper move? With restraint and the appropriate amount of power?

Golf also tests your decision-making ability. Can you make the correct choices under pressure to navigate various distractions, i.e., water, out of bounds, people, voices in your head, bunkers, etc.?

Golf tests your ability to overcome adversity. How do you respond when something bad happens?

Golf tests your honesty. Will you do the right thing even if no one is watching?

Golf tests you emotionally. Do you have self-control—especially when things get tough?

If you want to find out a person's true character, take him or her out for a round of golf.

Your Mind Turns into Mush!

See ya!

Golf screws with your head. Everything can be going really well and all it takes is one bad shot and that's it. The downward spiral begins.

You begin to question and doubt everything and lose all faith in what you've learned and practiced.

Eventually your brain says, "I'm outta' here. You're on your own!"

You find yourself standing on the tee or over a putt, eyes glazed over, mumbling to yourself and having no idea where the next shot is going.

The Mental Challenge!

Golf is not a reflex sport. In tennis and other fast-paced sports you instinctively react to what is happening around you in a split second. Perhaps golf would be easier if it were like that.

In golf there is a great deal of time between shots to think, worry, doubt, and conjure up imaginary mental demons that try to destroy your score.

Golfers of all levels, from club golfers to pros, wrestle with these same issues. The intense mental aspect of the game sets golf apart from most sports. Mental skills separate poor golfers from good golfers, good golfers from great golfers, and great golfers from tour pros.

There is nothing more satisfying than facing mental challenges and coming out victorious. It is how we grow as golfers and as humans.

Embrace the struggle. Eventually, you will prevail.

Dreams Are Crushed!

Each day you go to play golf you go with hope, anticipation, and excitement.

You say to yourself, "I'm with friends, the weather is perfect, and I'm playing a beautiful course. This is going to be a great day!"

Then shortly after you tee off, reality sets in. You're chopping it all over the course, and gradually your childlike enthusiasm turns to disappointment, then anger, then despair, followed by depression.

You now understand why golf courses have a 19th hole. After that round you're going to need a drink...or five.

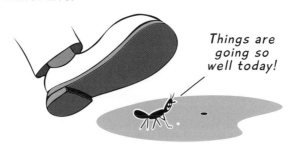

Things are going so well today!

How Will This Round Unfold?

It is impossible to predict how a round of golf will unfold. There will always be unexpected ups and downs, highs and lows, in a single round of golf.

That unpredictability is part of golf's beauty. You never know when something crazy is going to happen. You can be absolutely butchering a hole, staring double right in the face. Then out of the blue, you pitch one in from 60 yards to save par. Crazy game.

Other times you can be totally primed to play a great round and you get a bad break. Something you could never have anticipated happens and before you know it, your round is shot.

Golf, just like life, rarely goes as planned. The key to happiness in both is acceptance. Persevere, but also realize eventually crazy things, both good and bad, are going to happen to every golfer.

Everything Is the Opposite!

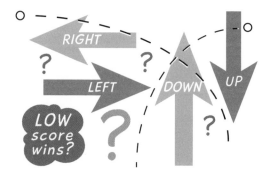

Nothing in golf is logical. It's like a cruel joke.

You try to hit the ball high and it goes low. If you want the ball to go to the left, you aim to the right. You aim right and the ball goes left. If you aim down the middle the ball *still* goes to the left or right.

You are supposed to hit the ball *before* the club hits the ground, unless you are in a bunker; then you want the club to hit the ground before the ball.

It is said that the key to golf is to try without trying *too* hard. What does that even mean?

It's Science and Logic!

The golf swing is a complex series of movements that, when broken down, are actually quite logical and easy to understand.

The key to success is to take time to learn the golfing principles of cause and effect.

Lack of faith is a big issue for most golfers; they don't trust that their equipment will do the job it is designed to do. This common problem is completely avoidable. If you relax and let the equipment do its job, you will have far more success.

Try giving up some control. Start by lightening up your grip pressure. You'll actually *gain* control!

Beyond technical adjustments, remember that you are human and therefore fallible. It's a given you will be less than perfect. Go easy on yourself. Embrace the process of failing and learning. Then everything about golf will begin to make sense.

The Scariest Word in Golf!

There is one word so hideous that it strikes fear in every golfer, no matter his or her skill level. This word is so terrifying that the mere mention of it on the course could start an epidemic. And once there is an outbreak, there is no telling when it will ever end. One thing is for sure: if there is one, there could be more—many more.

The word starts with "S" and ends with "hank."

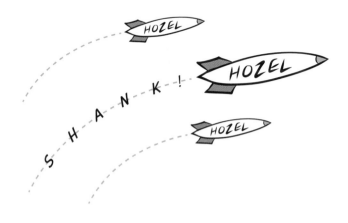

You Have My Deepest Sympathy.

Throughout this book, comparisons have been made about the things we love and hate about golf. In this case however, there is nothing to love.

When that A-hole S. Hank shows up, it isn't fun for anyone. Seeing a golfer completely overcome with fear, trying to summon the courage to draw the club back and swing, is tragic and sad. (It's even worse if it's you!)

Even if the infected golfer is your arch nemesis, watching him or her experience the terror, embarrassment, and hopelessness of hitting hozel rockets will make you completely sympathetic. That poor desperate soul. If there's anything good about the bastard S. Hank, it's the feeling of empathy that helps us remember that at our core we are all golfers and somehow, we are all in this together. All you can say is, "I'm thankful that it isn't me this time."

Side Effects!

The following side effects disclaimer should be posted on the first tee of every course:

WARNING: Golfing side effects include: pain; irritablility; involuntary jerking of arms, legs, and torso; temporary Tourette's syndrome; nausea; irrational behavior; having to go frequently; inability to make sound decisions; embarrassment; desire to drink (a lot); feelings of dread followed by sudden euphoria; depression; suicidal thoughts; inability to add; talking to oneself; sudden urges to break or throw things; paranoia; nervousness; and for some reason, loving every minute of it.

Face It, You've Got a Problem!

Golf isn't just a game, it's a lifestyle. A wonderful vice. A glorious disease. Embrace it!

Once golf infects you, it becomes a part of you. Need proof? Answer a few simple questions: Have you ever bought equipment and kept it from your spouse? In your car, do you have a sudden urge to pull over whenever you pass a golf shop? How often have you actually said, "Golf course!" out loud while passing one in your car, almost driving into a ditch because you were craning your neck to see as much of the course as possible while speeding by? When flying in a plane, what are the first landmarks you try to locate while looking out the window? Do you have a golf-related item on your office desk?

Let's be real. You are an addict and you LOVE it!

Say it! "My name is _____. I am a golf junkie." Sorry to inform you, most don't ever recover.

When Will I Get There?

It seems golfers, no matter their level, complain about the state of their game. Few seem to be satisfied with where they currently are, and if they are happy, they're only a bad round or two away from being dissatisfied once again.

When do you get there? Where is the finish line? Is there such a place?

It's About the Journey!

The wonderful thing about golf is that it gives every golfer new challenges each and every day.

The fact is, you'll never get there. Like life, golf is a long journey filled with ups and downs. There will be periods of great success and other times when you wonder why you ever took up this crazy game.

You will learn wonderful, useful lessons, some of which you'll forget and have to learn all over again.

The important thing about golf and life is to enjoy all of its moments—even the tough ones. You'll learn a lot about yourself and your game, and what needs to improve during the lean times. That is when the game is trying to teach you something valuable. There isn't much to learn when things are going smoothly, so just enjoy those rare times.

Decide to view your bad times as learning opportunities. Enjoy the journey.

It's Like You're Helpless!

Is golf a sickness? Is it some sort of twisted fetish? Why is it that you can play golf your entire life and still lose all your balls in one round? Day after day you leave the course angry or feeling worthless, and for some reason you can't wait to come back the next day and do it all over again.

Thank God for Golf!

Count yourself blessed that you were bitten by this thing called the golf bug.

Golf is a perfect and beautiful game to play for a lifetime. Anyone can play it *and* enjoy it! Golf favors no one. You don't have to be big or tall or slim or young. Even the disabled can play. You can begin swinging a club as a toddler and as long as you are mobile and willing, you can play until your last day.

Golf is a game that helps keep families close, links generations together, honors the past, and teaches invaluable life lessons to everyone who plays.

There aren't many sports that allow people who are separated by a half century the opportunity to compete as equals and to also share common experiences, problems, and goals.

Golf will always evolve, but its challenge remains the same—to get the damn ball in that damn hole.

About the Author

Golf humorist Fred Fruisen is a teaching professional and Class A member of the PGA of America. His instructional articles have been published both in the US and internationally in newspapers and magazines, as well as on his popular website: *coachofgolf.com*.

A former university head golf coach with a successful 18-year career, Fred also happens to be an award-winning illustrator and graphic designer.

Although his sense of humor has gotten him into trouble from time to time, some consider him to be a pretty funny guy. Fred is happily married, according to his "current" wife of 21 years.

Fred is currently living and teaching golf in Auckland, New Zealand.

Acknowledgements

Fred Fruisen is available for speaking engagements, corporate outings, golf clinics, or private instruction. He is also available for writing or illustration for publication. Feel free to contact him through his website:

Fred Fruisen, PGA

– Thanks to all my former golfers at SCAD who put their hearts and souls into turning a bunch of artists into a collegiate golfing powerhouse.

– Thanks to my lovely wife. Yes, I irritate you daily, but I hear that is how pearls are made.

– Thank you to Mauricio for having the faith in me to take on this entire project. I know it was a giant leap of faith. Hopefully, we both land in a giant basket of feathers.

About punchline

punchline is an imprint of duopress that
is dedicated to the delivery of content
with a fresh and novel approach.

We believe that life should be looked at from all
angles, and you should have fun in the process.

Hopefully, you like what we do.
We already like you for reading this!
www.punchlineideas.com

punchline books are available at special discounts
when purchased in bulk for sales promotions
as well as for fund-raising or educational use.

Special editions can be created to specification.

Contact us at
hello@duopressbooks.com
for more information.

If you like this book...

...please share the things that *you* love and/or hate about golf! Feel free to contact Fred Fruisen through his website, ***coachofgolf.com***; alternately, visit this book's Facebook page: ***Golf, I love/hate you***. If you can relate to any of the situations or people described in *50 Reasons to Hate Golf and Why You Should Never Stop Playing!*, we'd love to know!

"Golf is a puzzle without an answer."

— Gary Player